The Reflections of My Schnoodle

A Coloring Book

DOGGY LANGUAGE

There's an entire language devoted to dogs; this language is known as Doggo Lingo. It's how your dog speaks and thinks. It's a fun, positive celebration of dogs.

Doggo	Doggos come in a variety of sizes ranked by the size of their bork (bark). They range from the tiny yapper to a diminutive pupper, an average-sized doggo, and the biggest woofers and boofers.
Longboi	A long-bodied dog such as a greyhound.
Floofer/Fluffer	A very fluffy dog such as a Samoyed or Pomeranian.
Thicc boi	A chubby dog – more to love.
Smol boi	A little yapper.
Woofer	A big dog.
Loaf	A dog, slightly overweight, which resembles a loaf of bread.
Pupper	A puppy.
Heckin' bamboozled	Sometimes you bamboozle the dog, sometimes the dog bamboozles you. Heck.
Do me a frighten	When a doggo is worried , scared or confused, potentially in the presence of borks or woofers.
Doin' me a	Having an action performed on oneself.
Bamboozle	A deceiving trick.
Awoo!	Howling.
Hooman	A human being.

DOGGY LANGUAGE

Heck, h*ck	The curse work in doggo lingo
Blep/Blop	When your pupper is tired and his tongue hangs out just a little bit.
Mlem	Doing a lick. Not to be confused with a gentle blop.
Bork	Barking his little head off. All doggers can bork.
Boof	Not quite a bork, not quite a sneeze; it's the small huffy sound of a dog who's getting ready to bork..
Maximum borkdrive	This is otherwise known as the zoomies, when your doggo is going so fast they're just a blur.
Chimken	Chicken.
Fren/frend	Friend
Henlo	Hello
Snoot	The nose always knows, and the snoot was made for booping.
Boop!	Touching your pet on the nose. Frequently accompanied by saying 'boop!'
Good Boi	There are no bad boys.

Me and the hooman and the new fren went for a walk. And we saw other woofers and I jumped into a mud puddle. Awoo!

About My Dog

Dog's Name: ....

Date of Birth: ....

Breed: ....

Colour: ....

Gender: ....

Adoption Date: ....

Weight: ....

Breeder: ....

Microchip No: ....

Registration No: ....

Rabies: ....

Neutered/Speyed: ....

If you're lucky...

A Schnoodle
will come into your life,

...steal your heart
and change everything!

Some say a dog's life is easy...no worries, no taxes. I say, walk a mile in my shoes. That reminds me, I took your shoe.

SORRY, HOOMAN!

Photo

WE ARE AT THE PARK
BUT THE HOOMAN
SAYS IT'S
TIME TO LEAVE

THIS DOESN'T MAKE
SENSE BECAUSE
THEY CAN'T CATCH ME

AWOO!

My dog does this amazing thing where
he just exists and makes my whole life
better because of it

Hello frens.
Today has been a great day
to think about my
accomplishments.
Here they are.

ZOOMIES OF THE SPEEDY VARIETY
MAXIMUM SNOOZLES
CHASING BRUCE THE SQUIRREL
BORKED AWAY ALL EVILDOERS
ATE A WORM
SPAT OUT THE WORM
SNUGGLED WITH MY
STUFFED FREN, LEROY, ON
THE HOOMAN'S BED.

Dogs are like potato chips.
It's hard to have just one

The hooman yawned while having lunch, and in a split second, my floofer fren, Timbo, from next door stole a French fry. I AM WILDLY IMPRESSED!

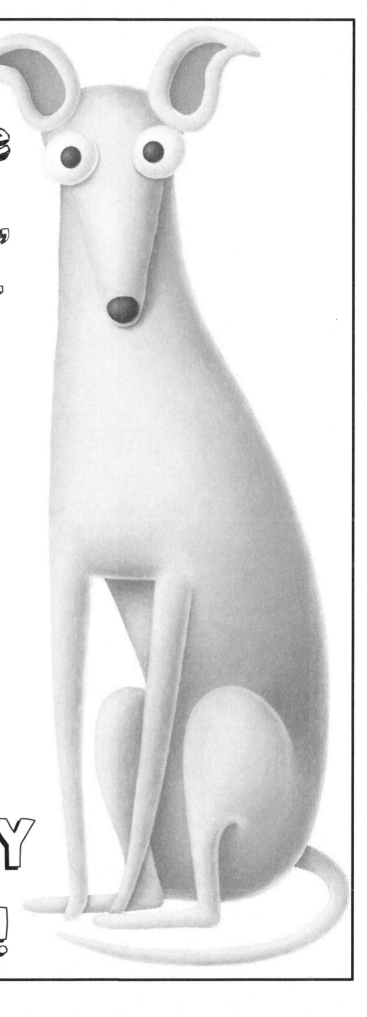

Dogs are God's way of apologizing
for your relatives

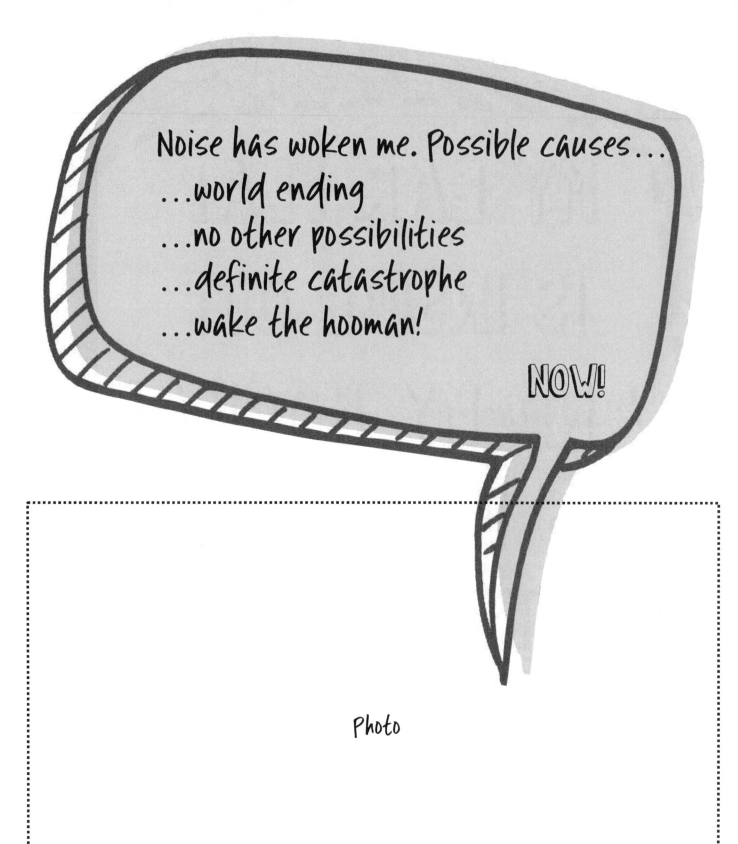

Photo

MY STUFFED FREN,
LEROY, IS A VERY
GOOD LISTENER.
I TOLD HIM ABOUT MY
IDEA FOR A DOG
COAT WITH BIG
POCKETS FOR CHIMKIN
AND PEANUT BUTTER.

HE SAID
THAT WAS
HECKIN'
BRILLIANT!

Dogs are the role model for being alive

JUST GIVE ME A LONG HALLWAY OF SHINY WOOD WITH SOME CHIMKIN AT THE END AND I'LL SHOW YOU SOME IMPRESSIVE SKATING

A dog does not think much about what he is doing.
He just does what feels right

Dogs have personality.
Personality goes a long way

The mailman left a box
at the front door
It smells like peanut butter

I'm trying my best
to remain calm,
but I think it's for me

GRR! AWOOOOO... BOOF!

IN HAPPINESS

A new week is upon us....
Or so the hooman tells me.
Hooman time constructs do me a
bamboozle. I prefer to break it down
into snoozes, non snoozes and.......

MAXIMUM BORKDRIVE

Photo

THE HOOMAN AND THE HOOMAN'S FREN HAVE GOT ALL DRESSED UP AND THEY'RE GOING OUT. I DON'T SEEM TO BE INVITED. THE GOOD NEWS IS, I JUMPED ON THEM BOTH, SO THEY HAVE PIECES OF ME TAGGING ALONG. AWOO!

I call my dog Egypt because he leaves
a pyramid in each room

We have new neighbors & they have a new pupper

I AM SO EXCITED!!

I shall take my stuffed fren, Leroy to make frens

MY TAILS A WAGGIN'

Dogs do speak but only to those who listen

MY SQUEAKER TOY, PAULINE THE PINK PIG, IS STUCK UNDER THE FRIDGE.

I AM HECKIN BAMBOOZLED ON HOW TO RESCUE IT

My little dog — a heartbeat at my feet

Guys, I just had a morning walk. Some big doggo borked at me and I almost caught Bruce, the lizard.

LIFE IS GOOD!

Photo

THAT PESKY CAT FROM NEXT DOOR SNUCK UP ON ME WHEN I WAS HAVING A SNOOZLE ON THE COUCH.

DID ME A HECK OF A FRIGHTEN!

GRR

I'LL BE READY NEXT TIME

Handle every situation like a dog.
If you can't eat it or play with it,
just pee on it

MANY HAVE TOLD ME
WHAT A GOOD BOI I AM

AND LET'S
SAY THEY
ARE
ABSOLUTELY
RIGHT

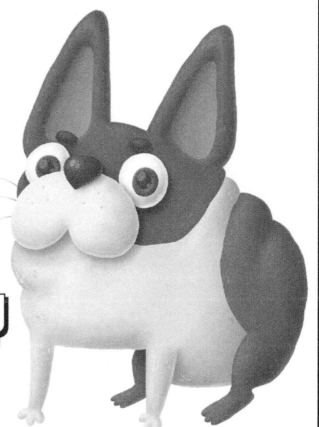

I'D LIKE SOME CHEESE
HOOMAN

No matter how many years we get
with our dogs, it's never long enough

The night snoozle
is here again.
I have gathered
my stuffed frens,
Leroy & Alistair
and they are safe in
the hooman's bed.

Lorem Ipsum

THEY ARE AFRAID OF THE DARK

Some days you're the dog;
some days, you're the hydrant

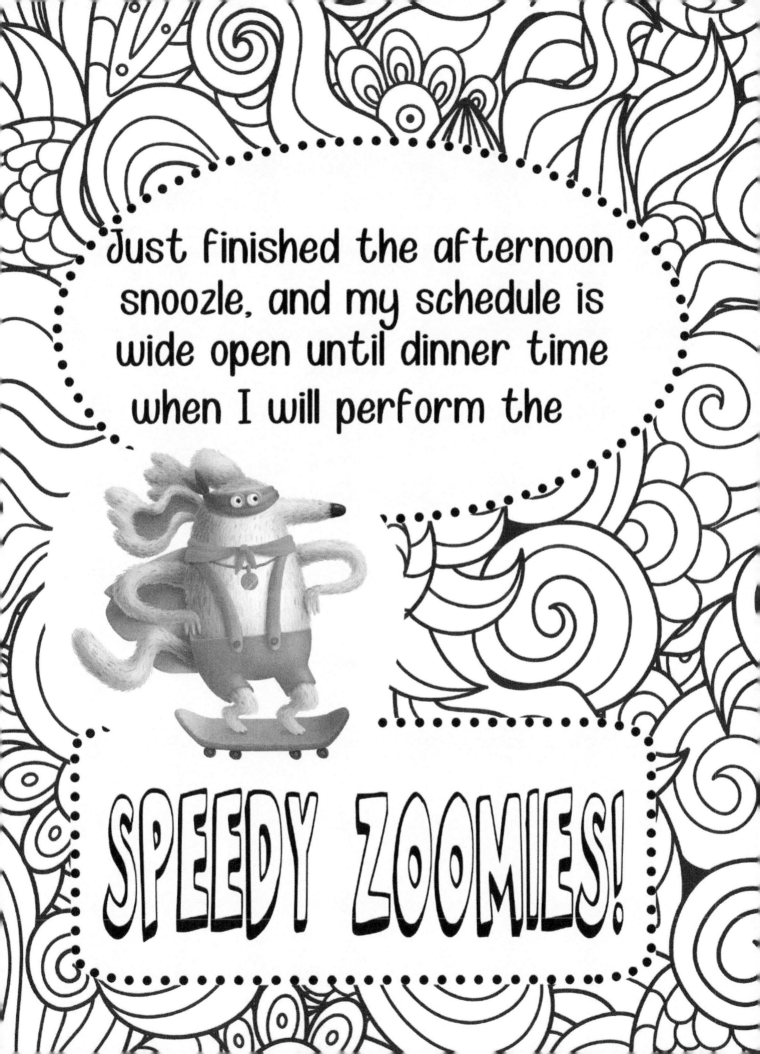

I have been programming my hooman. Every time they give me food, I bork. Eventually, every time I bork, they will give me food.

I WANT CHEESE!

Photo

I PRETENDED THAT I NEEDED TO GO THE BATHROOM

BUT I ONLY WANTED TO FEEL THE WIND ON MY NOGGIN

Every dog has his day, unless he loses
his tail, then he has a weak-end

I HAVE TWO
SPEEDS
FOR WALKING

FASTER THAN YOU
& COMPLETELY
IMMOBILE
(DRAGGING SPEED)

OF COURSE SOME
PEANUT BUTTER OR
A GOOD STICK
COULD CHANGE THAT!

Every snack you make, every meal you bake.
Every bite you take, I'll be watching you

I GOT THE MAJORITY OF MY WORK DONE... BETWEEN THE MORNING AND AFTERNOON SNOOZLES

But my hooman is cooking chimkin and I just know there will be some for me.

I wiggled a little bit....
just reminding her that
I am a good boi guard dog

My dog winks at me sometimes...
And I always wink back just in case
it's some kind of code

I am several hours
into my shift guarding
Pauline my squeaker pig

While I was there
the fridge made some
new crunch water

SOOTHED
MY
HECKIN
' BROW

Bruce, the lizard, is staring at me through the screen door. "Bring it on, young fella."

DOIN' ME A FRIGHTEN!

Photo

I wonder if other dogs think poodles are members of a weird religious cult

I JUST SAW SOME DOGGOS ON THE TV. I BORKED, GRBORKED AND BOOFED TO SHOW MY SUPPORT!

The great pleasure of a dog is that you may make a fool of yourself with him...

Dogs are such agreeable friends.
They ask no questions,
they pass no criticisms

MY HOOMAN HAS BOUGHT A NEW SOFA AND I'M NOT ALLOWED TO SNOOZLE ON IT.

I HAVE NO IDEA WHY BUT THIS SHALL BE REMEDIED

I WILL SLOWLY CLIMB UP ONE PAW AT A TIME.

NO ONE WILL EVER NOTICE!

Hooman gave me an extra long hug and direct eye contact. These are heckin' signals. We're on the same page.

I FEEL CHIMKIN COMING!

Photo

My sunshine doesn't come from the skies.
It comes from the love that's in my dogs eyes

MY HOOMAN IS HOSTING
A DINNER PARTY TONIGHT

AND it's MY JoB to
GReet ALL tHe Guests

CALMLY ... NO JUMPING!!!

THIS IS NOT POSSIBLE

I SHALL SEEK THE HELP OF
MY STUFFED FREN,
CHRISTMAS TURKEY

There is no psychiatrist in the world like a puppy licking your face

SOMETHING HAS WOKEN ME UP
IT'S THAT PESKY CAT, BORIS

I HAVE GATHERED
MY STUFFED FREN,
ALISTAIR THE CROCODILE
AND PREPARED
FOR EXTENDED SNOOZLES

A dog will always be happier to see you than any person ever will

I HEAR A DOGGO BORKING IN THE DISTANCE

It is my duty to respond so that all the other doggos know I heard the initial borking

IT'S JUST GOOD MANNERS!

The hooman said we could go on a car ride tomorrow when he gets home. I'm so happy, I can't even snooze.

TAIL IS WAGGING SO FAST!

Photo

If our dog doesn't like you,
we probably won't either

I HAVE MISPLACED
MY NEW FREN,
CHRISTMAS TURKEY

ALERT LEVEL
RED

NEVER MIND
I WAS LYING ON HIM
THE WHOLE TIME

ALERT LEVEL
GREEN

Don't let the dogs out
no matter what they tell you

A LOT HAPPENED ON OUR MORNING WALK

I found a perfectly good chimkin leg in the neighbor's trash, but the hooman wouldn't let me have it.

THERE WAS ALSO A VERY SCARY PLASTIC BAG

Dogs are better than humans because
they know but do not tell

THE HOOMAN BELIEVES HE HAS LOST HIS SOCKS IN THE SPINNY MACHINE

I BEG TO DIFFER

I steal them way before that

Hardwood floors are not ideal for doin' the zoomies. No traction anywhere. This situation needs to be remedied, hooman.

EAR FLAPS STUCK IN THE COUCH.!

Photo

I really love the sound of my dog snoring

I ACCIDENTALLY STOLE THE TOILET PAPER AND DECORATED THE WHOLE HOUSE

MY HOOMAN WAS WELL PLEASED !

Scratch a dog and you'll find a permanent job

I JUST WOKE UP FROM MY AFTERNOON POWER SNOOZLE

WHICH IS AFTER THE MORNING SNOOZLE

AND BEFORE MY NIGHT TIME SNOOZLE

I CAN'T KEEP UP WITH MY DAY!

My dog is half pit-bull, half poodle.
Not much of a watchdog, but a vicious gossip

DURING MY NIGHT TIME SNOOZLE I DREAMED THAT I DUG UP A BOX IN THE GARDEN & IT WAS FILLED WITH CHEESE

TODAY, I WILL TEST THIS OUT!

My most fancy tricks…
Snoozing, sit (a classic), the fetch,
trot/advanced walk, roll, zoom
(speedy), begging for chimkin.

SORTED BY DIFFICULTY!

Photo

I DRANK ALL THE WATER FROM MY BOWL BUT JUST NOW, IT IS FULL AGAIN

IT'S DOIN ME A FRIGHTEN

Everybody should have a shelter dog.
It's good for the soul

IF YOU HEAR A SINGLE **BORK** AND THEN A **BOOF** IT'S ONLY ME TESTING THE SAFETY OF THE HOUSEHOLD

Other doggos may respond & then we have a chorus!

If it wasn't for puppies, some people
would never go for a walk

Today, I did a zoom so speedy my ear flaps flew back

MY FLOOFER FREN FROM NEXT DOOR WAS WELL-IMPRESSED!

If you're uncomfortable around my dog,
I'm happy to lock you in the other room
when you come over

Sometimes, I grrbork at the sky... in case anybody is listening.
You ever wake up in the middle of the night and think...why?

I NEED CHIMKIN!

Photo

I COLLECTED ALL OF MY BALLS & SHOWED MY NEW FREN, LEON HOW TO HOLD THEM ALL IN HIS MOUTH

He's only little –
He could only do one

A dog has no use for fancy cars, big homes, or designer clothes. A stick will do just fine

SOMETIMES, MY HOOMAN WILL LIFT UP MY EAR FLAP AND SCRATCH MY NOGGIN

GYY

THIS IS COMPLETELY UNNECESSARY

When I needed a hand, I found your paw

Everyone thinks they have the best dog.
And none of them are wrong

Nobody ever told me that when you wake up from a snoozle, you can immediately start another one

I AM HECKIN' SMART

Photo

THE HOOMAN HAS A NEW FREN OVER.

IF I AM IGNORED, I WILL NOTIFY THE FREN WITH A SERIES OF DISCRETE BORKS

EITHER PAT MY NOGGIN OR GIVE ME PEANUT BUTTER

BORK BOOF GRR BORK

Dogs have a way of finding the people who need them, and filling an emptiness we didn't ever know we had

LET ME TELL YOU ABOUT MY BEST STUFFED FREN, JEREMY

HE'S MY BESTEST PAL

HE'S GOT A LONG SNOOT FLOPPY EAR FLAPS

HE AGREES WITH EVERYTHING I SAY

Whoever said that diamonds are a girl's best friend... Never owned a dog

MY TOP AGGRAVATIONS

BORIS, THE PESKY CAT

THE SPINNY MACHINE

LEASH TANGLES

CRUNCH WATER

INSIDE OUT EAR FLAPS

STICKS THAT BREAK

TAKE NOTE, HOOMAN

Some people don't understand
why my dog means so much to me.
That's ok. My dog does

If I am ignored, I will notify the hooman via a series of discreet borfs. The offender will then be removed from the house

IMMEDIATELY!

Photo

Stop telling me he's just a dog.
My dog has more personality, integrity,
empathy and loyalty than most people I know.
He's family!

I HAVE NO PLANS TODAY
JUST SNOOZLES AND SNACKS

I CANCELLED MY PLANS WITH MY FLOOFER FREN, TIMBO ABOUT HOW TO DO

MAXIMUM ZOOMIES

ON HARD WOOD FLOORS

A dog will always be happier to see you than any person ever will

DID I EVER TELL YOU

I love you hooman

Photo

Printed in Great Britain
by Amazon

12737593R00061